to ~~█████~~ + ~~█████~~

for

Christmas 2010

SUSSEX
Loving it!

GARY EASTWOOD

HALSGROVE

First published in Great Britain in 2010

Copyright © Gary Eastwood 2010

British Library Cataloguing-in-Publication Data
A CIP record for this title is available from the British Library

ISBN 978 0 85704 021 3

HALSGROVE
Halsgrove House,
Ryelands Industrial Estate,
Bagley Road, Wellington,
Somerset TA21 9PZ
Tel: 01823 653777
Fax: 01823 216796
email: sales@halsgrove.com

Part of the Halsgrove group of companies.
Information on all Halsgrove titles is available at: www.halsgrove.com

Printed and bound in China by
Toppan Leefung Printing Ltd

DEDICATION

I would like to express my gratitude to my wife, Victoria, for her unwavering support and help in the making of this book.

Cottages at Cuckmere Haven
A beautiful winter sunset casts an orange glow over the cottages of the tiny hamlet of Cuckmere Haven. The beach sits at the mouth of the Cuckmere River, which sets a meandering course through the reclaimed Cuckmere Valley.

INTRODUCTION

In the course of creating the images for this book, I have witnessed at first hand the true diversity, richness and beauty of the Sussex landscape; from misty sunrises atop downland ridges, to balmy dusks over peaceful river valleys, and brooding winter storms on clifftop headlands. But perhaps the most memorable moments were those spent enjoying the far-reaching views that stretch in all directions from many points along the majestic South Downs.

Admittedly, as a relative newcomer to the region – having relocated here just six years ago – I was still to be convinced of the beauty and drama of the Sussex landscape before the start of this project. But I stand well and truly corrected. The Sussex landscape has the capacity to bedazzle, beguile and inspire on a par with any location in the whole of Great Britain.

The South Downs are undoubtedly the jewel in the Sussex crown. Forming a part of England's newest National Park (along with East Hampshire), the Sussex section of the park accounts for an area of over 1000 square miles. The Downs cut a 70-mile spine right through the middle of the counties; from the village of West Harting, near the Hampshire border, in West Sussex, to the iconic Seven Sisters in the East, where the chalky cliffs drop vertiginously into the English Channel.

Inland too, the South Downs form an omnipotent and brooding presence, always lurking in the background, casting their influence over the surrounding countryside, and visible from many Sussex villages and towns, such as Midhurst, Petworth, Hurstpierpoint and Fulking.

Sussex, though, has so much more to offer than the Downs, from the sandy white beaches and secluded, reedy creeks of the protected Chichester Harbour, to the Victorian seaside resorts of Worthing, Brighton and Eastbourne. Not to mention '1066 country' around the Cinque Port of Hastings and the ancient towns of Rye and Winchelsea, Ashdown Forest, ancient chalk hill figures, medieval castles, Norman churches, canals, hill forts, snaking river valleys and flood plains … the list goes on.

Sussex is a land of rolling downland, soaring cliffs, stunning escarpments, peaceful river valleys, unspoilt towns and villages, sheltered inlets, bluebell-carpeted woodlands, dramatic ridges, and so much more. I hope this book manages to capture some of the essence of Sussex, and that I have communicated some of the sights, sunsets, dawns, views and moods that I have witnessed during the making of this book.

The images are presented in the 3:1 panoramic format, which I hope best captures the sweeping nature of this remarkable county. The choice of images is purely personal, and I acknowledge that this book represents my own unique vision of Sussex. But I have no doubt that others may have a different vision of Sussex, and in some cases may be disappointed that favourite locations and views have not been included. For that I apologise, but counter by suggesting that the sheer size, variation and content of the Sussex landscape would be too much to encapsulate within just a single book!

Farm buildings at Frog Firle
A lone cluster of farm buildings sits in a typical South Downs' scene of gently curving hills and mounds, criss-crossed by footpaths and bridleways. The valley of Frog Firle sits a few miles outside the picturesque village of Alfriston.

Yachts under purple dusk
Moored yachts cast their reflections across a still Bosham Channel, itself reflecting the purple and magenta colours of a lingering winter dusk. The hills beyond signal the start of the rise towards the South Downs around Chilgrove.

Dawn over Lewes Castle
A golden sunrise warms the town of Lewes following a cold winter's night.
The castle, built in Norman times, sits proudly overlooking the picturesque
market town, and can be seen from various vantage points in the area.

Petworth in yellow
The historic town of Petworth perches above bright yellow fields of rapeseed, which dot the Sussex countryside in spring and early summer. The large building in the centre of the picture is the rear of Petworth House, made famous by the oil paintings of JMW Turner, and its Capability Brown-designed landscape.

Snowdrifts at Devil's Dyke
Heavy snowfall and high winds have created unusual snowdrift shapes and transformed the iconic Devil's Dyke beauty spot into a winter wonderland. A glorious sunset adds to the drama of the scene.

Sunrise in Ashdown Forest
A farmhouse and its accompanying row of trees are silhouetted against a misty winter sunrise in the Ashdown Forest. With spring still around the corner, the bare trees create skeletal patterns against the purple dawn.

Cloud shadows over Beachy Head
Cloud shadows race across Beachy Head cliffs and headland on a clear
but breezy evening. The famous lighthouse is viewed from Belle Tout
lighthouse, which sits at the top of towering chalk-white cliffs.

Golden Arundel

Early morning sunlight bathes Arundel Castle in an orange glow, set against dark clouds in the background. In the foreground, gentle ripples on the River Arun create distorted reflections of this classic view of the Norman castle.

Autumn colours at Ditchling Beacon
Rows of trees bear autumnal foliage and colours, and form curving patterns and shapes at the foot of Ditchling Beacon, a well-known local viewing spot on the South Downs Way.

Dawn over The Chattri
The Chattri war memorial sits overlooking the city of Brighton in an isolated and poignant location on the edge of the South Downs. The Chattri was erected in memory of Indian soldiers who lost their lives in the First World War.

Norman church at Upwaltham
Broken clouds part briefly to bathe the tiny 900-year-old church of St Mary the
Virgin, in Upwaltham, in bright sunlight. The small hamlet nestles in a valley in the
South Downs National Park, halfway between Chichester and Petworth.

Flooded Amberley meadows
The River Arun on the outskirts of Amberley, a village at the foot of the Downs near Pulborough, bursts its banks following months of wet winter weather, turning surrounding fields into temporary lakes.

Dusk at Cowdray
The ruins of Cowdray House on the outskirts of the West Sussex market town Midhurst, hint at this country house's former glories. Cowdray sits within its own grounds on the banks of the River Rother.

Vanishing point
The village of Steyning is completely submerged by thick fog on a winter morning, viewed from
the top of Steyning Bowl. The 'bowl' refers to a deep, circular valley with steep sides, while the
tip of Devil's Dyke and the surrounding Downs escarpments are seen in the far distance.

Spring beckons at Bodiam
The impressive walls of Bodiam Castle are reflected in the waters of its moat on a peaceful spring morning. The castle, situated near Robertsbridge in East Sussex, has gained iconic status among photographers and visitors alike.

Moored yacht at East Head beach
A yacht lands at the peaceful sandy cove of East Head, which is a part of the West Wittering conservation area for migratory birds. Set within Chichester Harbour, the clear waters, white sand and sheltered sand dunes of West Wittering make it a popular tourist destination.

Long Man of Wilmington
View of the Long Man of Wilmington on a spring evening. The ancient human figure is cut into the chalky slopes of Windover Hill, part of the South Downs between Lewes and Eastbourne.

Sunset over Halnaker
Halnaker Windmill sits on a hilltop overlooking Chichester and the South Coast. Here, an impressive red sunset silhouettes the windmill against a sky of fluffy clouds.

View over Hastings Old Town
A hazy winter sunset turns the sky orange in this view over the rambling streets of Hastings Old Town, as seen from the town's East Hill. Hastings is one of the famous Cinque Ports on the English South Coast.

Frosty morning at Seven Sisters
A frost-covered track leads towards the tiny hamlet of Cuckmere Haven at the
mouth of the Cuckmere River, and provides a view along the famous Seven Sisters
cliffs and South Downs' coastline towards Belle Tout lighthouse in the distance.

Twisted trees at Chanctonbury Ring
A gnarled tree provides the foreground for this view north from the ancient hill fort of Chanctonbury Ring. The South Downs are seen stretching away north-eastwards towards Truleigh Hill and beyond, as the sun rises on a frosty winter's morning.

Ancient bridge at Stopham
Early morning mist rises from the tranquil waters of the River Arun, underneath the Elizabethan stone bridge of Stopham. The bridge, between Pulborough and Petworth, was built as a replacement for an ancient timber bridge which stood on the same spot.

South Harting vista
Looking north on a clear evening from the top of Harting Downs towards the village of South Harting, which lies close to the border of West Sussex and Hampshire.

Purple dusk at Bosham
A high tide quickly recedes in Bosham Harbour, viewed here from the village of Chidham on the opposite side of the inlet. Some roads in old Bosham village are partially flooded each high tide.

Sunlit beach huts at Wittering
A strong wind blows sand across the dunes of West Wittering, while golden evening sunlight illuminates the beach huts lining the popular beach at the mouth of Chichester Harbour. Hayling Island can be seen in the distance, while travelling east in the opposite direction leads to the broad, sandy expanse of Bracklesham Bay.

Broken clouds at Bostal Hill
Scattered clouds scud across a blue sky in this view from Bostal Hill, near Firle, looking north and east over the village of Alciston and along the edge of the South Downs towards Windover Hill.

Brighton's West Pier in snow
This scene of the much-photographed ruins of Brighton's West Pier is made unusual by a heavy snowfall over previous days, crowned by a wonderful winter sunset.

Atmospheric Pevensey Castle
A misty morning provides eery atmospheric conditions for this view along the walls
and moat of Pevensey Castle. The medieval castle stands on the same spot as a
Roman fort, which was built to protect Roman conquerors from Saxon attacks.

Harvest at Poynings
A lush, late-summer, English country scene surrounds the village of
Poynings, set at the foot of Devil's Dyke on the South Downs near Brighton.

Bleak winter on Seven Sisters
A bleak winter scene on top of the Seven Sisters headland is lifted by a glowing, pink sunset. The scene was shot in a break between ominous, snow-laden storm clouds.

An Eastbourne evening
A lone bench provides sweeping views over the seaside resort of Eastbourne, which has the honour of being the sunniest place in Britain. The town is viewed from the slopes of the white cliffs that continue to rise westwards towards Beachy Head.

Beauty at Belle Tout
Sheep graze on the fertile headlands of the Seven Sisters cliffs in this view from the outskirts of the village of East Dean towards Belle Tout lighthouse.

Dawn colours over Alfriston
A misty winter dawn casts yellow and purple colours over the picturesque village of Alfriston, in the Wealden distirct of East Sussex, as the sun climbs over the surrounding slopes of the South Downs

Slindon Folly in evening sunlight

A gravel track winds its way past the the Folly in late-afternoon sunlight on the Slindon Estate, which is located in the Arun district of West Sussex

Ruins on Harting Downs

The ruins glow red in a sunset over the northern flanks of the South Downs, near Harting in West Sussex. On a clear day, the area offers far-reaching views in all directions, north to the Weald, south to Chichester, and east towards the Isle of Wight.

Chalk cliffs at Burling Gap
The undulating chalk cliffs of Seven Sisters, seen here from Burling Gap, reflect the golden afterglow of dusk, as waves gently lap against the pebbly foreshore. Seaford Head juts into the Channel in the distance.

Fishing boats on Hastings beach
The sun rises over beached fishing boats in the East Cliff area of Hastings Old Town. The beach-launched fishing fleet is Europe's largest and respected for its sustainable methods.

Classic Cinque Port
Fishing boats line Rye Harbour in this classic view along the quay looking towards the famous Cinque Port in the far east of Sussex.

Balcombe Viaduct shrouded in mist
The Balcombe Viaduct, which carries the main London-Brighton train line across the River Ouse
Valley, sits shrouded in a veil of mist as the morning sun tries to break through low-level cloud.

Autumn scene at Jevington
An autumn evening highlights the gold and red colours in the countryside around
Jevington, a small village nestled in the South Downs near Eastbourne.

Jack or Jill?
The Clayton Windmills, known locally as 'Jack' and 'Jill' (background and foreground, respectively), are set
on the South Downs above the village of Clayton, and afford splendid northerly views across the Sussex Weald.

Reflections on Alfriston
A flooded field casts reflections of Alfriston church, in the Wealden region of the South Downs. The picturesque nature of Alfriston attracts many visitors to the market town.

Dusk over Crowlink
A stone seat provides the foreground of this dusk view over the Seven Sisters cliffs towards Seaford, as viewed looking west from Crowlink.

Berwick village and surrounds
The church spire of Berwick protrudes from the misty,
rolling landscape of the Wealden South Downs.

Sand dunes at Climping
The grasses of Climping sand dunes blow in the breeze under a dusk of wispy clouds. The beach, near Littlehampton, contains rare vegetated shingle and remains an undeveloped part of the Sussex coastline.

Volcanic sunset over Windover
Icelandic volcanic ash in the atmosphere provides a technicolour sunset in this view looking
West over Firle Beacon and the South Downs from the top of Windover Hill in East Sussex.

Edge of the Cuckmere Valley
A boundary fence drops sharply down into the River Cuckmere Valley in this view south towards Cuckmere and the mouth of the river, seen from 'High and Over' hilltop.

Sunset over Chidham
Looking west along a launch ramp at Bosham quay towards the village of
Chidham and beyond into the sheltered inlets of Chichester Harbour.

View to Cuckmere Haven
The stiff climb up Haven Brow at the beginning of the Seven Sisters cliffs is rewarded with glorious views over Cuckmere Haven beach towards Seaford Head Nature Reserve.

Cobbles at Keere Street
The cobbled Keere Street in Lewes curves down a steep hill
and offers glimpses of the South Downs in the distance.

Still waters at Chichester marina
Rows of moored yachts cast reflections on the still waters of Chichester marina on a clear
spring evening, one of several marinas within the Chichester Harbour conservation area.

Swans on the Cuckmere River
Two swans enjoy a frosty, but peaceful, dawn on the River Cuckmere, under the shadow of the chalk carving of a White Horse in the slopes of 'High and Over' in East Sussex.

Red, gold and blue at Seven Sisters
Sheep graze near a bright red barn on the snow-covered clifftop above the
East Dean estate in East Sussex. A colourful winter dusk paints the sky beyond.

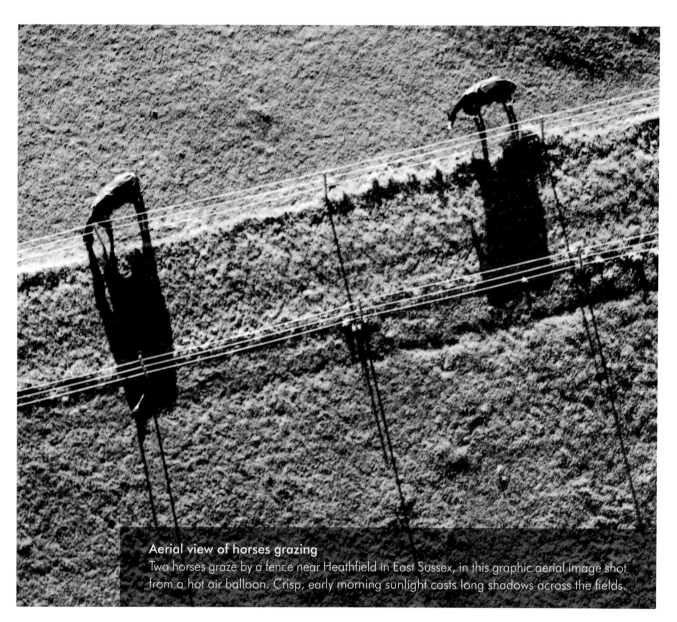

Aerial view of horses grazing
Two horses graze by a fence near Heathfield in East Sussex, in this graphic aerial image shot from a hot air balloon. Crisp, early morning sunlight casts long shadows across the fields.

MERELY PLAYERS

For Pete,
Liz —
& family
with love —
Bobbie Hanvey
5 August 02 . x

Portraits from Northern Ireland
by Bobbie Hanvey

Edited by Brian Turner

8 7 6 5 4 3 2 1

ISBN 1 898392 55 2 Casebound

ISBN 1 898392 56 0 Paperback

Layout and design: Colourpoint Books
Cover design: Barry Craig at Colourpoint
Printed by: W & G Baird Limited

Cover: Seamus Heaney, poet, wearing his father's hat.

Colourpoint Books
Unit D5 Ards Business Centre
Jubilee Road
NEWTOWNARDS
Co Down
BT23 4YH

Tel: 028 91 820505
Fax: 028 91 821900
E-mail: info@colourpoint.co.uk
Web site: www.colourpoint.co.uk

Dedicated by Bobbie Hanvey to

Rosemary, Viscountess Brookeborough
Maurice Hayes
Brian Turner
David Hammond

ACKNOWLEDGEMENTS

We are very grateful to David Hammond for his fair criticism and encouragement given freely to Bobbie throughout his career. In producing this book we are particularly grateful to Aidan Flanagan, Louis Fredlander, Claire Grimes, and Geoff Martin.

Down District Council, through its arts service and Down County Museum, encouraged the promotion of Bobbie's work; Deirdre Armstrong and staff at Library Headquarters in Ballynahinch helped with information; Jenny Woods of KJP in Belfast helped with the supply of Ilford and Kodak film, and Hasselblad UK have been generous with the equipment with which most of the photographs have been taken. Our publishers, Colourpoint Books, have managed the difficult task of being both exacting and pleasant.

In a project such as this, one conversation leads to others, often by unexpected routes. This journey round our friends, neighbours, fellow citizens and visitors has taught us a lot. We thank them all, and we hope that this picture of Northern Ireland people will stimulate the imagination of those who see and read it.

Note on captions
Words printed in italics in the captions are direct quotations from the photographer.

Bobbie Hanvey, born in County Fermanagh in 1945, lives in Downpatrick, County Down. He has won many awards as a press photographer, and his work has been exhibited at Down County Museum and widely used in Ireland, Britain and north America.

Brian Turner, born in Cork in 1946, is Director of Down County Museum. He has written and lectured widely on local history and culture and is a member of the Northern Ireland Museums Council and the International Committee for Regional Museums.

INTRODUCTION

"Why have Jews got such big noses, Louis?"

"Because they know the air is free. And you have a big nose yourself, Bobbie."

"Irish Catholics think the air is free – but we all have a sneaking feeling that we'll have to pay for it sometime."

This snatch of conversation between Bobbie Hanvey and Louis Fredlander (page 90) catches the photographer's mixture of curiosity, outrageousness, and self-knowledge. He says that his motivation for taking photographs is a desire to record history. He has done that, both in the course of his work, and for curiosity and 'crack', throughout the troubled generation leading up to the millennium in Northern Ireland. He did not want to take 'snaps' of people, but to make photographic studies of individuals who may normally be thought of in terms of over-simplicity and caricature.

But there are paradoxes. Despite his interest in history, Bobbie Hanvey is not an historian. He comes from a different tradition created, I think, in the world of the peasant, whose priority is to deal with each day as it comes, and to snatch any advantage which presents itself. Most of us in Ireland have this in our background, sometimes for good, and sometimes not. In Bobbie's case I think it is the characteristic which has enabled him to support himself by his self-taught skill in photography, and which is very useful in developing an acute sense for an opportunity. The opportunity can be manipulated by the photographer, as in the photograph of Ian Paisley beside the statue of Lord Carson at Stormont (page 10), which involved using mechanical hoists, or it can simply be the wit to grab an instant which causes us to ponder (page 23).

Bobbie Hanvey was born in Brookeborough, County Fermanagh, on 31 October 1945. The fact that his birthday is at Hallowe'en is, he maintains, the reason why he has always liked eating apples and putting his head into basins. This basin habit was taken a stage further in the 1980s in rural County Down when he decided to mark the anniversary of the death of the Australian bushranger, Ned Kelly, who wore home-made armour, by re-enacting his final shoot-out and execution with a bucket on his head.

Bobbie's father, Johnny Hanvey, came from Doran's Rock, near Saintfield in County Down, and his mother, Mary Donnelly, was from Colebrooke Cross in Fermanagh. The father went to Fermanagh before the Second World War to direct teams of men cutting down trees on the great estate of Colebrooke and others in west Ulster. Bobbie's maternal grandfather served in the Cameronian Highlanders during the Boer War, and had two brothers who emigrated to join the New York Police Department, and who were both shot dead during a stakeout in 1910, only a year after joining the force.

Johnny Hanvey must have been unusual for a lumberjack in rural Ireland in the 1940s and 50s, for he took photographs of the men and machines he worked with. And he bought his teenage son a tape recorder. Bobbie used his father's camera to photograph his neighbours, and the tape machine to record their songs and ceilis. True to his tradition he saw life through the people who lived it, and related to him. "I wouldn't be interested in photographing hills or anything like that."

When asked about the major influences on his life Bobbie Hanvey always mentions his father, and people in Brookeborough. His father's gifts of a tape recorder and a camera "are the things that have kept me alive right up until now." Indeed they have. Apart from his photographic business Bobbie's programme on Downtown Radio, 'The Rambling Man', is based on interviews with people who catch his interest, ranging from clergy to gunmen to novelists, and has been running for twenty-two years. His style can be both subtle and direct: "Well Joe, tell me about the time you did the heart-transplant on the chicken."

Johnny Hanvey died on the day that the Northern Ireland government at Stormont was closed in 1972. "All the shops were told to shut. A Protestant neighbour, Tommy Ovens, had a shop across the street. His brother was the police Sergeant Ovens killed during the IRA's 1956 campaign. He came over to my mother. 'The shop's closed', he said, 'but you come over and take everything you want for the wake.' And there was no charge. But during the wake another neighbour came and asked to speak to my mother. She went out to him and he said, 'How much would you want for Johnny's greenhouses'. And my father not even in the ground! And this man was trying to buy his greenhouses! That taught me to be careful, to observe, to know that people are not always what they seem."

After jobs in textile factories in Enniskillen and Lisnaskea, and the summer of 1965 singing in folk clubs in England, Bobbie came back to Northern Ireland and somebody told him that psychiatric caring was a good job. After failing to get a job at the Mental Hospital in Omagh he applied to the Downshire Hospital in Downpatrick. He had no qualifications. "No papers, like a good dog." But this time he had prepared well for the interview. "Can you play the guitar?" he was asked. "Yes", he said. "You've got the job", they said.

In addition to music therapy one of the charge nurses in the Downshire hospital took ciné-film of the patients for their

Johnny Hanvey and his son, Bobbie, in the back yard of their Brookeborough home, 1948.

entertainment. Bobbie started to help, and took still photographs. Two other nurses at the hospital showed him how to develop and print them, and somebody else taught him about cameras. He got books about photography and a dark room, and stayed in it until he understood. In the early 1970s he went full-time as a general photographer, recording weddings, babies, news items, and retaining an interest in music by taking photographs for record covers. In 1985, 1986, and 1987 he won the Northern Ireland Provincial Press Photographer of the Year Award for himself and the *Down Recorder* newspaper of Downpatrick. In 1985 and 1987 he also won the Northern Ireland overall award for 'Best People Picture'. These were the only three years that he entered the competitions.

Since then he has carried on his solo business and, in his spare time, consciously recorded the faces of those he found interesting.

Until now there has been no collected publication of Bobbie Hanvey's work. His public photographs have usually been seen in newspapers or on book and magazine covers. In 1998 the Hulton Getty Picture Collection used ten of his images in *The Irish Century* (Weidenfeld and Nicolson). Previously, in 1996 and 1998, Down County Museum held exhibitions of his work in Downpatrick, based on the theme of 'priests, poets, politicians, and paramilitaries', and subsequently acquired a representative cross-section of the collection. As Director of the museum the reaction to this exhibition confirmed my view of its current social value as well as its artistic and historical significance. At the formal opening of the exhibition people from all parts of our community literally rubbed shoulders, including those who might readily have killed each other in a different setting. They saw people they probably hated as well as those they admired. But they joined the photographer in simply observing. It may seem like a modest ambition in Northern Ireland, but it chimes with what I believe to be the radical purpose of our museums, which is to be common ground where people can meet without fear, not to escape, but to consider the difficult questions of our past and present, and to find their place.

This collection can, if the reader wishes, have a powerful purpose. It asks you to consider the humanity of Northern Ireland. It contains no underlying structure of artificial 'quotas' by which we might try to achieve equally artificial 'balance' in the selection of people included. It is simply a view, taken through the collection of this photographer and those he has had the opportunity to photograph. Its purpose is not to give biographical information, but to stir consideration of the faces you see, and of the others whom they represent. Its range is necessarily limited within the variety of human experience but it refers, not only to the famous or notorious, but to those who quietly live their own lives, sometimes achieving much more than those who make greater noise. Here is the paradox again. While the observer can see the 'mere players' on the stage, there comes a time to remember that we share the stage, and to wonder how our play will end. Each individual is different, and deserves more than a glance or a prejudiced dismissal. So do Ireland and Northern Ireland.

As the twentieth century closes, many of the elements of Irish history in the previous millennium are still with us, developed, twisted, wonderful, courageous, shameful, dangerous, and hopeful. You can hear them all playing softly behind the names and faces in this book.

Brian S Turner
Lisban, Saul, County Down.
August 1999

THE PORTRAITS

All the world's a stage,
And all the men and women merely players

William Shakespeare
'As You Like It'

Charles Fitzgerald, arts journalist and critic.
He really is the last of the Mohicans. He reminds me of Mr Sandeman, coming out of the Opera House in his hat and cape and riding off on his motorbike.

10

Rev Dr Ian R K Paisley, Member of Parliament for North Antrim, MEP.
This photograph, taken beside the statue of Lord Carson at Parliament Buildings, Stormont, won the award
for 'Best People Picture' in 1985.

Sergeant Sean Mooney, Royal Ulster Constabulary.

His Eminence Cardinal Tomás Ó Fiaich (1923-1990) at St Patrick's Cathedral, Armagh.

Victor McCarthy, agricultural contractor, ambulance driver, footman and chauffeur to three Governors of Northern Ireland.

Senator Maurice Hayes, public servant, writer and journalist.
Chairman of the Ireland Funds Advisory Committee; former Northern Ireland Ombudsman.

'Buck Alec' Robinson, and Gusty Spence.
Buck Alec was a loyalist militant and streetfighter in the 1930s, who at one time kept two lions 'Roger' and
'Sheila' in his Belfast back yard. (*He worked with Al Capone, you know.*) Gusty Spence was the Ulster Volunteer
Force leader imprisoned for nineteen years for murder in 1966. In the 1990s he announced a loyalist ceasefire.

James Chichester-Clark, Lord Moyola, last Prime Minister of Northern Ireland.

Harry Murray, Belfast shipyard shop-steward.
Chairman of the Ulster Worker's Council whose strike brought down the power sharing Northern Ireland
Executive in 1974. Later joined Alliance party.

Sam Hanna Bell (1910-1990), writer and broadcaster.

**His Eminence Cardinal Bernard Law,
Archbishop of Boston.**
The Cardinal surveys the scene from
Sliabh Padraig in the Parish of Saul,
County Down, where tradition says
that St Patrick began his mission to
Ireland.

**Mary McAleese, university administrator, later President of the
Irish Republic.**

Joe Cahill, veteran IRA man.
Reprieved from death sentence for killing a policeman in Belfast, 1942; sentenced in Dublin to three years penal servitude for gun-running and Provisional IRA membership, 1973.

Sam McLaughlin at his home in east Belfast, 1979.
As a young man he worked in Belfast shipyard as a rivetter on the *Titanic*.

Edith Kohner, retired businesswoman.
With her husband and children, a Jewish family, she arrived in Belfast from Czechoslovakia, via Germany, France and England, on 7 August 1939.

Gerry Adams, President of Provisional Sinn Féin, and Mairead Corrigan-Maguire, Nobel Peace Prize winner. Mid 1980s.
"Stop the murder, Gerry," she said. He thought for a second. Then he stuck out his hand. And she took it.

Ballynahinch bomb, 1985.
Scenes like this were repeated in many towns in Northern Ireland in the last third of the twentieth century.
I looked round the corner and saw it. I just couldn't believe it. It was so eerie and quiet.

Seamus Heaney, poet.

Basil Brooke (1888-1973), 1st Viscount Brookeborough. Prime Minister of Northern Ireland 1943-1963.
He asked me "How did you get past the security?"

Martin Meehan, Sinn Féin worker.
In Belfast on his 50th birthday he was presented with a bullet-riddled sheet of corrugated iron. The reference was to a gun battle between the Provisional IRA and the British army at Dungooley Cross on the Armagh-Louth border in January 1972. The only casualty on that occasion was a pig – which was in the middle.

James Kelly, journalist and political analyst.

James Hawthorne, Controller of BBC Northern Ireland 1978-1987.
Former Director of Broadcasting Hong Kong; Chairman Community Relations Council and Chairman Health Promotion Agency.

Gerry Fitt, Lord Fitt of Bell's Hill, and his mother Mary Ann.
MP for West Belfast 1966-1983; leader of the Social Democratic and Labour Party 1970-1979.
He worked night and day for people – brought them into his own house – and the same people forced him to leave the country!

Rev Sydney Callaghan, Methodist Minister.
Founder member and later Director of The Samaritans in Northern Ireland.

Pastor Bob Bain of Mountain Lodge Pentecostal Church, Darkley, County Armagh, preaching at Scarva.
On Sunday 20 November 1983 republican gunmen walked into his church firing at the congregation.
Three were killed, seven were seriously injured.

Raymond Piper, artist.

Gregory Campbell, Democratic Unionist Party representative, Londonderry.

Sir John and Lady Sylvia Hermon.

Sir John Hermon, Chief Constable of the Royal Ulster Constabulary 1980-1989.

Mary Hamilton, rural cultural activist.
The next project begins, behind – the Dooneen Cultural Education Centre, County Fermanagh.

Colin Crichton, owner of the *Down Recorder* newspaper.

Rev Roy Magee, Presbyterian minister.
Ceasefire broker between government and loyalist paramilitary organisations.

Rev Canon Bernard Magee, Parish Priest of Loughinisland, County Down.
He has a bullet in his head, you know.
Canon Magee survived an attempted assassination in east Belfast in 1974.

John Bryans, aged 101.
Methodist lay preacher; Past Grand Master of the Grand Orange Lodge of Ireland.
He told me "Always go to your place of worship".

James Cahill (1897-1987). The Master.
Schoolmaster in Teconnaught, County Down.

The McElroys of Drumnaquoile, and Kevin Cunningham on accordion.
Traditional musicians.

Paddy Devlin (1925-1999), socialist and writer.

Roy Hall on the Old Grand Jury Road, Saintfield 1986.
He always carried the bag. I asked him, "Roy, what do you carry in the bag?" "Groceries," he said.

Rosemary, Viscountess Brookeborough.
She keeps telling me "Bobbie, you really are a disaster".

Seamus Deane, poet and critic, professor of Irish Studies.

James Molyneaux, Lord Molyneaux of Killead; leader of the Ulster Unionist Party 1979-1995.

Brian Friel, playwright.
He writes with a 2B pencil. Did you know that?

Andy Tyrie (right), Supreme Commander of the Ulster Defence Association (1973-1988), and his deputy John McMichael.
John McMichael was assassinated by the Provisional IRA in 1987.

John Hume, MP, MEP, Leader of the Social Democratic and Labour Party.

The Most Reverend Lord Robin Eames, Archbishop of Armagh, Primate of All Ireland.

T P Murphy, Secretary of the Down County Board of the Gaelic Athletic Association 1962-1990.

'Blackmen' at the field, Scarva, County Down.
On 13 July each year the Royal Black Institution has a demonstration in the grounds of Scarva House.

Damien Gorman, poet.

Jenny Woods, photographic store manager, and Jaffa.

Eddie McGrady MP and Kerry Kennedy, daughter of the late US senator Robert Kennedy, in Downpatrick, 1988.

D J Hawthorne (1913-1996), founder of the *Mourne Observer* newspaper, County Down.

Ruairí Ó Brádaigh, former Chief-of-Staff of the IRA, President of Republican Sinn Féin.

John Lowe, road sweeper, Carryduff, County Down.

Brush with the law.
When faced with this situation one day in the mid 1980s, Constable Logan of the RUC's Mobile Support Unit had been on continuous duty for 48 hours.

David (left) and Nick Lindsay, company directors.

Patrick Forde and the Lady Anthea Forde of Seaforde, County Down.

John White, Ulster Democratic Party representative.
Former Ulster Freedom Fighters prisoner, sentenced for the murder of Senator Paddy Wilson and Irene Andrews in 1973; subsequently adopted political role.

Jonathan Taylor, solicitor.

Rex McCandless (1915-1992), inventor.

Beryl Holland (1903-1999), campaigner, and Democratic Unionist Party councillor.
She couldn't understand why anybody would want to photograph her – but Dr Paisley gave her the mug.

Punks on the street, 1986.

Claire Grimes, publisher of the *Irish Echo*, New York.
Visiting from 'the States' and photographed near Annalong, County Down.

Rev Hugh Ross, Independent Ulster movement.

Baz Titterington, company director.

Margaret Barry, 'Queen of the gypsies', with Dominic Behan, Dublin singer and songwriter.

Rev Ruth Patterson, first woman ordained in the Presbyterian Church in Ireland.

John Campbell and Patrick McKinley, storytellers, south Armagh.
McKinley used to make prophesies, but he started to get so accurate he scared himself and had to stop.

Enoch Powell, Member of Parliament for South Down 1974-1987.

Philomena Begley, 'Queen of Irish country music'.
Did you ever see her on stage? She really commands attention.

Billy Hutchinson, former Ulster Volunteer Force prisoner, Progressive Unionist Party representative.

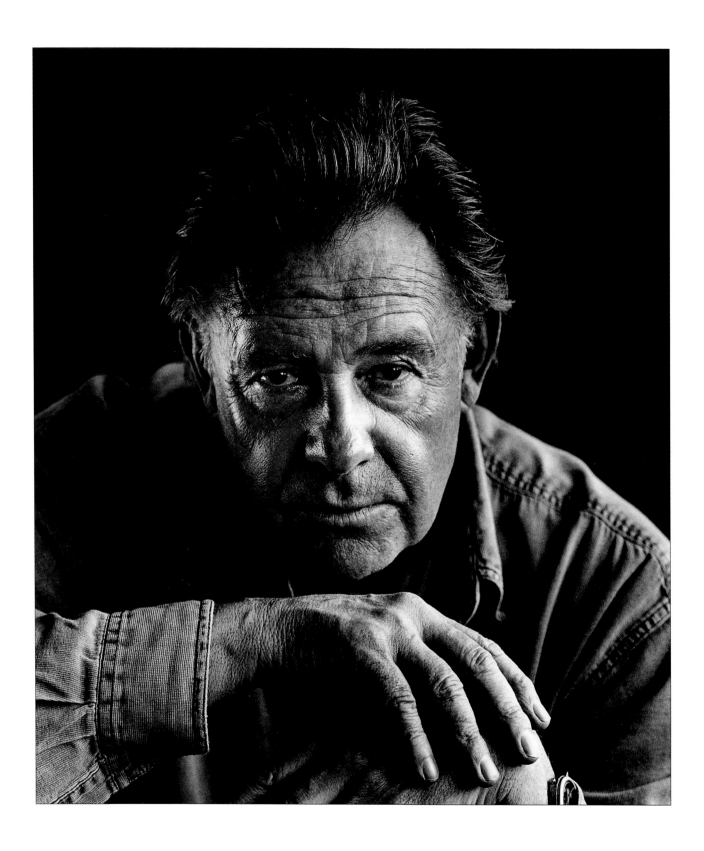

Maurice Leitch, novelist.

Walking home. Divis flats, Belfast.

Leonora, Countess of Lichfield, and Miss Lavinia Baird of Belle Isle.
Conversation at a wedding reception in Fermanagh, 1989.

Christiane Amanpour, Chief International Correspondent, Cable News Network.
Whenever she's around, the shutters are down.

Christopher Napier, solicitor.

Malachy McGrady, accountant and public servant, and Mrs Collette McGrady.
Photographed after being instituted as a Knight Commander of the Order of St Gregory the Great.

John B McGuckian, businessman, County Antrim.
Former Chairman of the International Fund for Ireland.

Lambeg drummer, South Derry.

Ruth Dudley Edwards, historian.

Willie Chambers (1917-1991) of Tullynaskeagh, County Down, farmer.

Sir John Gorman, former
presiding officer of the
Northern Ireland Assembly.

Joan Bullock of Aghalane, County Fermanagh, conservationist.

Michael Longley, poet.

Candy Devine, radio presenter, jazz singer, and actress.

Neil Shawcross, painter.

Louis Fredlander, Belfast businessman.

Don O'Doherty, broadcaster, raconteur, concert artist and promoter.

Sir Donald Murray, retired judge of the Supreme Court of Northern Ireland.

Eamonn McCann, concert promoter.
Organised a huge concert in the Waterfront Hall, Belfast, in 1998, at which Bono, lead singer of rock band U2, raised the hands together of John Hume and David Trimble, as a symbol of the desire for peace.

Sean Mahon, businessman.
Formerly trombonist and trumpet player with The Freshmen showband.

Rebecca Brown, Private Investigator.
She's very good at disguises.

Wallace Clark, soldier, sailor, and linen manufacturer.
I think he has the nicest voice I ever recorded.

Neil Johnston, *Belfast Telegraph* **arts correspondent.**

Traveller children.

**Sir Oliver Napier, Leader of the Alliance
Party 1972-1984.**

Geoff Martin, editor of the *Newsletter*.

Major William Brownlow (1921-1998) with bronze sculpture of 'Master McGrath'.
One of Major Brownlow's forebears was the 2nd Lord Lurgan who owned the Irish sporting hero which won the
Waterloo Cup in 1868, 1869 and 1871.

    Lord Lurgan stepped forward and he said 'Gentlemen,
    If there's any among you has money to spend,
    For you nobles of England I don't care a straw,
    Here's five thousand to one upon Master McGrath.'

General Sir Roger Wheeler, Chief of the General Staff; Aide-de-camp General to the Queen.
First commissioned into the Royal Ulster Rifles, 1964; General Officer Commanding and Director of Military
Operations, Northern Ireland, 1993-1996.

Billy McBurney, record producer and distributor.

Gerry Kelly, television presenter and chat-show host.

Gordon Wilson (1927-1995) and Mrs Joan Wilson.
Gordon Wilson's demonstration of Christian faith and fortitude when describing the death of his daughter, Marie, in the Enniskillen Remembrance Day bombing in 1987, in which he was injured, is an outstanding memory for many people. He accepted a seat in the Irish Senate in the hope that it would 'help to build bridges'.

Dignity and grief.
Mrs Vera Hazlett, daughters, daughters-in-law, and other relatives watch the funeral of RUC Inspector Jim Hazlett as it passes the home near which he was assassinated in Newcastle, County Down, April 1986.

Cathal McConnell, traditional singer and musician.

Terence Flanagan, painter.

David Hammond, singer, folklorist and film maker.

John Taylor MP, Deputy leader of the Ulster Unionist Party.
In 1972 he survived bullet wounds to the head in an assassination attempt by the Official IRA.

Peter Jones, barrister.

David Trimble MP, Leader of the Ulster Unionist Party.

Monsignor Denis Faul, Headmaster of St Patrick's Academy, Dungannon.

Alistair Simpson, Governor of the Apprentice Boys of Derry.

Jack Johnston of Clogher, County Tyrone, local historian and farmer.

David Jones, spokesman for the Orangemen of Portadown at their Drumcree demonstrations in County Armagh.
The signpost is at Drumcree, County Westmeath.

Catherine McCullough, Curator of Armagh County Museum.

Danny Morrison, writer and critic.
At the 1981 Provisional Sinn Féin Ard Fheis he said, "with an armalite in one hand and a ballot paper in the other, we will take power in Ireland". In 1990 he was sentenced to eight years in gaol for unlawful imprisonment of another person.

Gerry Anderson, broadcaster and struggling author.
He invented the name Stroke City for his native place, ie 'Derry stroke Londonderry'.

Henry Robinson, former paramilitary turned human rights campaigner.

Niamh McMorrow, student.

His Eminence Cardinal Cahal B Daly, Archbishop of Armagh (1990-1996).

Desmond Tutu, Archbishop Emeritus of Cape Town, South Africa.
Archbishop Tutu visited Northern Ireland in the cause of reconciliation in 1998; "...goodness will ultimately prevail".

William Rutherford, Consultant in the Accident and Emergency Unit of the Royal Victoria Hospital in Belfast, 1967-1986.
Can you imagine it!

Sarah-Anne Hanvey and her gerbil.

Harry West, Minister of Agriculture in the former Stormont government; leader of the Ulster Unionist Party 1974-1979.

Give me a real dour Protestant look, Harry. And he did. I said, practice makes perfect. And he roared laughing.

INDEX